# The Scapular of Carmel

# The Scapular of Carmel

Very Rev. E. K. Lynch, O. Carm.

With Preface by Cardinal Francis Spellman

AMI Press
Washington, New Jersey

Nihil Obstat
Romæ, 20 januarii 1955
Kennetus Leahy, Censor Dep.

Imprimatur
E Vicariatu Civit, Vatic., 1 martii 1955
Fr. Canisius van Lierde, Ep. Porphyr.
Vic. Gen. Civ. Vat.

1996 Edition

Printed in the United States of America

**World Apostolate of Fatima
Washington, New Jersey
07882-0976**

ISBN 0-911988-11-4

TO MY MOTHER
WHO FROM MY CRADLE-DAYS
TAUGHT ME
TO LOVE
THE "MOTHER OF FAIR LOVE,
OF KNOWLEDGE AND OF HOLY HOPE"

# Contents

Publisher's Note .................................. ix
Letter of Pope Pius XII on the Seventh Centenary
    of the Brown Scapular ......................... x
Preface by Cardinal Francis Spellman ............... xii

*Chapter One*
The Origin of the Brown Scapular .................. 1

*Chapter Two*
The Spiritual Significance of the Scapular ............ 7

*Chapter Three*
A Pledge of Everlasting Salvation ................... 15

*Chapter Four*
The Sign of Our Perfect Consecration to Mary ....... 25

*Chapter Five*
Our Affiliation with the Order of Carmel ............ 32

*Chapter Six*
The Carmelite Way ............................... 38

# Publisher's Note

We are grateful to the Very Rev. E. K. Lynch, who wrote this book when he was the prior general of the Carmelite Order.

Father Kilian, during his generalate, restored the ancient Priory of Aylesford where the Blessed Virgin appeared to St. Simon Stock. The author arranged the return to England of the major relics of St. Simon Stock from Bordeaux where the saint died at the end of the thirteenth century. Subsequently, Aylesford has become the most popular Marian shrine in England.

In 1964 Pope Paul VI clarified the Second Vatican Council's general endorsement of Marian devotions, citing the Rosary and the Scapular as specific examples.

This booklet, first published at Aylesford in England, is one of the best brief presentations of the story and meaning of the Scapular.

We are deeply grateful to Fr. Kilian Lynch and the Carmelite Fathers for permission to reprint it in the United States.

All scripture references are taken from the Douay-Rheims Bible.

# Letter of His Holiness, Pius XII, For the Occasion Of the Seventh Centenary Of the Brown Scapular

To our Beloved Sons, Kilian Lynch, Prior General, and Silverio de Santa Teresa, Master General, of the Order of the Most Blessed Virgin of Mount Carmel

There is no one who is not aware of how greatly a love for the Blessed Virgin Mother of God contributes to the enlivening of the Catholic Faith and to the raising of the moral standard. These effects are especially secured by means of those devotions which more than others are seen to enlighten the mind with celestial doctrine and to excite souls to the practice of the Christian life. In the first rank of the most favored of these devotions that of the Holy Carmelite Scapular must be placed—a devotion which, adapted to the minds of all by its very simplicity, has become so universally widespread among the faithful and has produced so many and such salutary fruits.

Therefore it has pleased us greatly to learn of the decision of our Carmelite brethren, both Calced and Discalced, to take all pains to pay homage to the Blessed Virgin Mary in as solemn a manner as possible on the occasion of the Seventh Centenary of the Institution of the Scapular of Our Lady of Mount Carmel. Prompted therefore by our constant love for the tender Mother of God, and mindful also of our own enrollment from boyhood in the Confraternity of this same Scapular, most willingly do we commend so pious an undertaking and we are certain that upon it will fall an abundance of divine blessings. For not with a light or passing matter are we here concerned but with the obtaining of eternal life itself, which is the substance of that promise of the Most Blessed Virgin which has been handed down to us. We are concerned, namely, with that which is of supreme importance to all and with the manner of achieving it safely. For the holy Scapular, which may be called the habit or garment of Mary, is a sign and a pledge of the protection of the Mother of God. But not for this reason, however, may they who wear the Scapular think that they can gain eternal salvation while remaining slothful and negligent of spirit, for the Apostle warns us: "In fear and trembling shall you work out your salvation" (Phil. 2:12).

Therefore all Carmelites, whether they live in the cloisters of the First and Second Orders or are members of the Third Order Regular or Secular, or of the Confraternities, belong to the same family of our Most Blessed Mother and are attached to it by a special bond of love. May they all see in this keepsake of the Virgin herself a mirror of humility and purity; may they read in the very simplicity of the garment a concise lesson in modesty and simplicity; above all may they behold in this same garment, which they wear day and night, the eloquently expressive symbol of their prayers for the divine assistance; finally may it be to them a sign of their consecration to the Most Sacred Heart of the Immaculate Virgin, which (consecration) in recent times we have so strongly recommended.

And certainly this most gentle Mother will not delay to open, as soon as possible, through her intercession with God, the gates of heaven for her children who are expiating their faults in purgatory—a trust based on that promise known as the Sabbatine Privilege.

Now, therefore, as a pledge of the divine protection and help, and as an assurance of our own special dilection, we most lovingly impart to you, beloved sons, and to the whole Carmelite Order, the Apostolic Benediction.

*Given at Rome on the Feast of the Apparition at Lourdes, February 11, 1950.*

# Preface

Holy Mary, Mother of God, Gate of Heaven, Mother of mankind, pray for us; deign to enfold us within thy mantle; be for us a shield from sin and from the agony of sorrow which sin has wrought upon the world; grant unto us, O beloved Protectress, the blessing and joy of peace on earth and everlasting peace in thy Son, our Divine Redeemer, the Prince of Peace!

As history unfolds under the watchful eye of Divine Providence, God sets signs in the sky "at sundry times and in divers manners." This He does with the loving care which a Shepherd is wont to lavish on his sheep as He guards and guides the human race in its onward march to destiny. In olden ages the sign was a cloud by day, a pillar of fire by night. In later centuries it was the Cross brilliantly set against the sky, revealing to mankind the message of God's love and his mercy. Then, in years close to our own day, He sent to us at Lourdes, LaSalette and Fatima, his own Blessed Mother!

And never was man's need greater for guidance and help from merciful Mary than it is in this decade of postwar sorrow and despair. Therefore must we daily pray that never again will man, in the lust and hate and sin of war, barter his birthright of peace for unjust power and greedy gain. United in mighty faith and love we must beg of Mary intercession with her Son Divine, that He, Who from our confusion and disorder fashioned beauty and design, will once again come to the world's salvation: enliven men with love, quicken them with truth, inspire them with justice, instill within them mercy, that peace may come to dwell within their hearts and reign supreme on earth.

Like unto the gentle rains that fall from out the heavens unto earth there to nourish the seed of flower and of fruit, like unto the light and warmth of day that stream from sun to earth to nurture every creature on it, so God-given glories of grace flow to us through Mary, merciful Mother of mankind, who alone can bring us to Christ as she brought Christ to us. And He, our King of Kings, will save us and the world, if we but go to Him through Blessed Mary. For she who knew his heart better than all others; she who understood Him as no other understood; she alone will grant us intercession, if faithfully we prove our love of Him in prayers devout.

The saints, martyrs, confessors and virgins, the angelic choirs and all the hosts of heaven, blend through hymns of praise with ours, when we acclaim Mary, Queen of Heaven and of Earth. Our prayers and theirs echo in heart-swelling melody through the archways of heaven, as we bow in loving veneration, praying for guidance, protection and peace before our Queen and Mother, enthroned at the right hand of Christ her Son. For in God alone dwell the power and the promise of peace. In man alone abide the wit and will to seek or reject it. Who but ourselves can choose the road we take? Who but God shall lead us? Who but God Himself and Mary can tell us the myriads of prayers flung in ceaseless chants and pleadings at the feet of our Mother in heaven, there to break in sprays of petitions like the waves of a mighty sea? Thence, through the flow of time, these, our prayers, surge back to us in a wealth of graces, representing God's love for Mary, and through her holy heart, for all mankind.

For the occasion of the seventh centenary of the institution of the Scapular of Our Lady of Mount Carmel Father Kilian Lynch has written this book which tells of the mission of Mary as Mother of mankind, explaining the mystic meaning of the Brown Scapular, the badge of identity of the children of Carmel and the sign of the pact between the Mother of God and God's devout children. Mary pledges to protect them. The pledge to profess her, as they wear the little brown mantle—Mary's mantle—with which she covers and protects her children.

It is the precious privilege of the Carmelites, and the members of their Confraternities to have an especial spiritual kinship with Mary, and I pray that *all* Mary's children in this Holy Year of 1950, will promise more deeply to love her and follow in her footsteps and the footsteps of Jesus Christ, Mary's Divine Son and our Redeemer. To Christ through Mary, his Mother, we must daily pray for peace, for we, who know Mary's-might and her mercy, know we need not fear for the future, if with faithful, trusting hearts we implore her powerful intercession. Neither flood, nor fire, nor famine, neither death, nor war, nor slavery, can perish the people of the earth, if in faith and love they will unite in prayer to Christ, our Savior through Mary, his Virgin Mother.

Therefore in daily passioned prayer that fervently bespeaks our everlasting faith in God, united let us lift our souls, beseeching Him through Mary, Mother of mankind, to grant us peace!

> What is a mother? Who shall answer this?
> A mother is a font and spring of life,
> A mother is a forest in whose heart
> Lies hid a secret ancient as the hills,
> For men to claim and take its wealth away;
> And like the forest shall her wealth renew
> And give, and give again, that men may live.
> A mother is a forest in whose trees
> The breath of God makes melodies all day,
> While in the night she shelters in her breast
> The weak, the timid, the oppressed of earth.
> A mother is a song begun in spring
> Deep'ning in summer and in autumn filled
> With life's rich meaning and exalted truth.
> A mother is a song flung from God's lips
> When all the world was mirthful at its dawn,
> And echoes still his love across time's vale.
> A mother is God's image here re-cast
> And fairer now in Mary than in Eve—
> The second casting has a flawless grace,
> The second flowering a white rose.
> We turn to Mary in her motherhood,
> And ask of her that which her love concedes,
> A mother's ceaseless care for one and all,
> That men may find Christ's hand before too late,

May touch with Thomas his faith-giving wounds,
May know with Magdalen conversion's joy,
And come at last into that holy place,
The kingdom built by a Father's love,
And sealed with the dear blood of his own Son,
And graced by Mary for her children's rest
When, in good time, this night shall be no more.
And kneeling humbly before her we pray
O Mary, Mother of mankind,
Our intercessor be unto thy Son,
Lift us to Him, bring down God's peace to us.

>+ Francis Cardinal Spellman
> Archbishop of New York, New York
> May 12, 1950

*Chapter One*

# The Origin of the Brown Scapular

It is no exaggeration to say that the scapular devotion is as universal as the Church. It would be difficult to find a Catholic who has not at least heard of it for, as Pius XII says, it is in the "first rank" of popular devotions to the Blessed Mother. And yet how many there are who know little or nothing about the origin of the scapular.

Like many good and holy things that have come down to us from the past, the scapular (to be understood properly) has to be seen in the light of its historical setting; to take it away from the century of its origin is to deprive it of a great deal of its significance and to rob it of its value as a religious symbol.

Since the rise of monasticism, a scapular, consisting of two pieces of cloth joined at the shoulders and hanging down back and breast, has been a part of the monastic habit. The fact that it hung from the shoulders immediately suggested a spiritual meaning, for Christ spoke of the faith in terms of a burden to be carried. "My yoke," He said, "is sweet and my burden light." As the monk rose in the morning to begin a new day, the putting on of the scapular reminded him that he had taken the sweet burden of divine service upon him and that the day ahead was to be all for God.

When one is acquainted with the desire of the Church that

we put our faith into our daily lives and sanctify even the little things of life, one can easily see how the wearing of a scapular could be a strong incentive to faithful and generous service in the vineyard of the Master. Even the sight of it could be a reminder of a promise made but easily forgotten by the ordinary person.

The birth and ascendancy of the mendicant orders served to strengthen the spiritual significance of the religious habit of which the scapular was the principal part. Coming as it did in the thirteenth century, the friar movement was bound to be affected by the feudal system which was then at its height. The friars were, by profession if not by origin, poor men who identified themselves with the poorer classes and worked among them. Their habit, even though similar to that of the monk, was that of the common folk. It was inevitable that the relation of vassal to lord that dominated the whole economic, social and political life of the Middle Ages would affect their religious outlook and that the timeless relation of creature to Creator would be expressed in terms of it.

Living as we do in an age very different from that of the Middle Ages, we find it hard to visualize the dependence of the vassal upon his lord. While feudalism held sway, it was a matter of life and death to belong to a lord. Before the rise of towns, commerce and industry, land was the only means of livelihood; and since it belonged to the lord, one had to have the right to till it in order to live. The vassal's act of homage gave him the right as well as that of protection, which was as important then as it is now.

Knowing how much faith and actual living were one in the Middle Ages, one can see how feudal ideas influenced religious ideas and practices and how the habit, of which the scapular is the principal part, took on a new meaning. Being a man of God, the friar was keenly aware that God is our one and only Master but, after the manner of the time, he presented himself before his Divine Master as the vassal presented himself before his lord "to pay his homage" and to receive the investiture from his hands. The religious ceremony of receiving the habit, although different in meaning, was the same as that of feudal investiture. Just as the vassal placed his hands in or between his lord's and pronounced his oath of fealty or homage, so did the friar present himself before a superior, who took the place of God, to make his vows. The scapular, hanging from the shoulders, was an outward sign that the friar was "God's man," that he belonged entirely to Him and that he would pay Him the homage of his whole life.

It is in this medieval setting that one must see the Brown Scapular that is the habit of the Carmelite friars in miniature form. Before they entered the European scene, the Carmelites were a group of hermits living on Mount Carmel in Palestine. They believed themselves to be the spiritual sons of Elias the Prophet, and the life they led on Mount Carmel was patterned on his life of contemplation. The Elian tradition, however, was not the only one to influence them, for, long before they came to Europe, they were known for their devotion to God's Mother. So devoted were they to her that they became known as the "Brothers of Our Lady of Mount Carmel," a title they cherished and defended down through the years. The earliest documents we have bear eloquent witness to their love for Mary; for in her they found the fulfillment of the Elian ideal. She, too, kept all the things that God said to her, pondering them in her heart and making her life their incarnation; and it was by following her that they found the clean heart that sees God even in this life. When they made their profession, they vowed their lives to God and to her, and it was in her honor that the homage of their lives of contemplation was offered to their Lord. Mary was the Queen and Mistress of the holy mount; Carmel was her land, her vineyard, where they worked in the hope of her guidance and protection.

As a result of the Saracen invasion the Carmelites finally decided to leave Mount Carmel. It was a difficult decision to make for their ancient home had many memories for them. An old tradition holds that before their departure Our Lady appeared to them as they were singing the *Salve Regina* and promised to be their Star of the Sea. Fortunately they found staunch friends among the Crusaders who brought them with them on their return journey to Europe. Some settled in Cyprus, others in Italy, while others continued their journey to France and England. The English group found a benefactor in Lord de Grey, who gave them Aylesford in Kent.

Although the Carmelites found many favorably disposed to them in the West, they also encountered much opposition, so much so that, about the middle of the thirteenth century, it seemed as if their days were numbered as an order. However, in 1246, at a Chapter held in Aylesford, they elected Simon Stock as their General. As he saw the waves of opposition mounting higher and higher, Simon realized that Our Lady was his only hope. The habit he wore spoke for itself for it was in her honor he had taken it. It had always reminded him that he was hers, and the long years of his life were an act of homage to her. Carmel was not his but hers; and now that it was in danger of being destroyed forever, he went to her as the vassal would go to his lord and asked her to give it her protection. Saluting her as the Flower of Carmel and the Star of the Sea, he asked her for the "privilegium," that is, the protection a lord would give his vassals. In answer to his fervent prayer she appeared to him, and giving him the scapular of his order she said: "This shall be a sign to you and to all Carmelites: whoever dies wearing this shall not suffer eternal fire." The promise Mary attached to the scapular went far beyond Simon's expectations. It saved the order, confirmed its Marian character and made Mary more a Mother than a Queen to it.

One has merely to glance at the history of the order from the thirteenth century down to the present to see how the scapular vision served to strengthen its devotion to Mary. And the external sign of that love and devotion through the years has been the Brown Scapular.

Some people are inclinced to exaggerate the importance of visions and private revelations and in assessing the spiritual value of the scapular devotion one must keep in mind the teaching of the Church regarding them. It is the constant teaching and practice of the Church that devotions must be founded on revealed truth and that visions and private revelations have relative value only; they serve to focus attention on some truth God has revealed and must be interpreted in the light of it. The popular devotion to the Sacred Heart is not based on the revelations to St. Margaret Mary but on the Incarnation of the Word. The same must be said about the Lourdes and Fatima devotions. The visions of Our Lady called attention to her role in the economy of redemption and to the old Christian doctrine of prayer and penance.

It is in this context that one must see the scapular devotion. It is based on the spiritual motherhood of Mary in the setting of Carmelite history. The total dedication of the order to her made the scapular a sign of consecration to her. And what more fitting sign could one find of her spiritual motherhood than a garment. When she brought forth her Firstborn she wrapped Him up in swaddling clothes and it was she who wove the seamless garment by which He was known. The Carmelite habit has always drawn minds and hearts to her and been a sign of her loving protection.

For a long time the habit was the exclusive property of the order, a sign of profession in it and of the life totally consecrated to her but in the fourteenth century we find a bridge appearing between Carmel and the world. Pious people living in the world became anxious to live its Mari-form life and to share in its spiritual treasury of prayer and good works; and as a visible sign of their affiliation to the order they were given the scapular. This was the beginning of the third order of Carmel and of the confraternity. These good people were often generous benefactors and in return for their help the order granted them a share in all its Masses, prayers and good works. With the lapse of time this participation was given without any financial assistance.

Here we find the two essential elements of the scapular devotion. Consecration to Mary in Carmel and participation in the spiritual life of the order.

In a comparatively short time the wearing of the scapular spread to the whole Church and became the unmistakable mark of the good Catholic. Popes, kings, princes, nobles and humble folk alike lived and died in the hope of the promise made to St. Simon, and the scapular devotion grew to be one of the leading devotions to the Mother of God. As a Marian devotion it has stood the test of time, and the seven centuries that have elapsed since the vision have served to reveal its beauty. It has kept generation after generation aware of its duty to call Mary blessed, and in the homage paid to her, countless saints have come to realize that to find her is to find life in her Son and to draw salvation from Him.

*Chapter Two*

# The Spiritual Significance Of the Scapular

To know the spiritual value of the scapular one must see it not only in its historical setting but also in the light of the Marian life of the order to which it belongs. When isolated from the inner life of Carmel, the scapular loses much of its spiritual significance, for it is much more than a sacramental of the Church. This is exactly what has happened today. Millions are enrolled in it and wear it without ever knowing what it should mean to them in their daily lives. We hope that a presentation of its spiritual significance will bring more of the faithful to recognize it as the traditional sign of a life lived in, through, and with Mary.

It is evident that the Blessed Mother wishes to call our attention to the scapular, for Lucia, now Sister Mary of the Immaculate Heart, assures us that when Mary appeared to her at Fatima, she wore on one occasion the Carmelite habit and held the scapular in her hand. Sister Mary of the Immaculate Heart also tells us that Mary was never so beautiful as she was on that occasion. This latest expression of love for the habit of Carmel should focus the attention of the faithful upon it and bring all true lovers of Mary to wear it worthily.

From the beginning, the God Who dwells in light inaccessible has been pleased to accommodate Himself to our ways of thinking and acting. He spoke to Adam as man would speak to man, and taught him to see the supernatural in the ordinary things of life. The voice of nature is the language of heaven, and the invisible things of God are made known to us through the things we see, hear, taste, touch and smell.

In all his dealings with us, particularly under the Old and New Laws, we find God making use of a beautiful symbolism. The chosen people were educated to read the signs of his love and anger and to find his graces and blessings hidden in the humble things of nature.

When God became man we saw the glory of the Only-Begotten. He became one of us, like us in all things with the exception of sin. The Incarnation gave the human and the sensible a permanent place in the economy of our salvation. How human and how intelligble to us are the Nativity, the Crib, the years of toil at Nazareth, the privations of his public life, the agony in the garden and his death on the Cross! And yet, these incidents in the life of Christ reveal the infinite love of God that was hidden from all eternity.

In his relations with us God shows a preference for the simple things of life. What could be simpler than the manger of rough straw in which his life here below began! That same simplicity went with Him to the grave. When He willed to enrich our souls with the precious fruits of his Passion and Death, He instituted a sacramental system in which seven simple elements become the efficient signs of divine grace. Since the natural function of water is to wash, He chose it to show us what his grace does for the soul stained by original sin. Since bread is the staff of life, He chose it to reveal how the grace of the Eucharist nourishes our souls. The symbolism of the whole sacramental system is designed to lead us into the knowledge of what divine grace is doing in the hidden depths of our souls. It is a continuation of the divine condescension of the Incarnation and Redemption.

The spiritual significance of a simple garment is perhaps as old as human society itself. A garment has always signified something more important than itself. After the Fall, God clothed our first parents, and the garments He gave them were the sign of his forgiveness. Jacob made a coat of divers colors for his favorite son, Joseph, and Anna also made a coat for her son, Samuel. A garment was also the mark of that extraordinary friendship which knit the souls of Jonathan and David: "And Jonathan stripped himself of the coat with which he was clothed and gave it to David" (I Kings 18:4). The priestly vestments designed by God were an outward sign of the high office entrusted to the priests of the Old Law.

From the time of Elias, the prophet, a garment has had tremendous significance in Carmel. When the time came for the great prophet to retire from the spiritual combat of his day, God sent him to anoint Eliseus to be prophet in his place. And when Elias came to him, he cast his mantle upon him. Eliseus immediately understood the significance of the gesture for the sacred text adds, "and rising up he went away, followed Elias and ministered to him" (III Kings 19:21).

And when the time came for the ascent of Elias in the fiery chariot, his successor asked him to leave him his double spirit. Elias informed him that he had asked for a very difficult thing but promised it would be his; and as he ascended into the clouds his mantle fell upon Eliseus, bringing him the double spirit of his master.

St. Paul does not hesitate to call the human nature of Christ a habit. The Redeemer Himself compared grace to a wedding-garment, and the Apostle of the Gentiles loved to use the same metaphor of a garment when exhorting us to put on Christ and to clothe ourselves with his virtues.

The garment, perhaps, that has the greatest significance for us is the one made by the Blessed Mother for the Infant Jesus. We can easily imagine our Blessed Mother making the swaddling clothes in preparation for the birth of her Son; and when she set out for Bethlehem she made sure to bring them with her, that she might wrap Him up and lay Him in the manger. Later, during the quiet hours of Nazareth, she prepared the seamless garment He wore to Calvary. She was always mindful of her duty to clothe her Child, and we may be be sure that Christ's eye never fell upon the garments his Mother made for Him that He did not think of the love and the solicitude she had for Him. Our Blessed Lady's motherhood extends to all the redeemed. She is the Mother of the "whole Christ," that is, of the whole mystical body. The active part which her Son gave her in our regeneration made her the Mother of the life of grace that is in our souls. Before He died on the Cross, Christ proclaimed her our Mother; and one would almost expect her to have a garment for us.

For long years before she appeared to St. Simon, the habit was a sign of devotion to her. It was worn by the Brothers of the Order of Our Lady of Mount Carmel, who were known for their devotion to her. The Marian character of the habit was known to all and recognized by several popes in official documents.

The scapular itself is the simplest thing on earth; it is just two pieces of cloth worn over the shoulders. The mantle of Elias must have had a similar simplicity about it, but when it fell upon the shoulders of Eliseus it brought him the double spirit of his master. It was not the mantle Eliseus coveted but the spirit it brought him. The same may be said of the mantle of Our Lady; in itself it is worth no more than is the drop of water or the morsel of bread; its whole value consists in what it represents. Seven centuries of Christian devotion have helped to reveal the hidden treasures of the scapular. Saints have meditated upon it and scholars have studied it, but they have not revealed all its spiritual value.

The scapular is a sign of our special adoption by the Mother of God. The first and the greatest privilege it brings is that it envelops us in the special love of our Blessed Mother. It makes us "hers" in a very special way. She repeats to us the words of the prophet Ezechiel: "And I passed by thee and saw thee: and behold thy time was the time of lovers: and I spread my garment over thee and covered thy ignominy. And I swore to thee, and I entered into a covenant with thee...and thou becamest mine" (Ezech. 16:8). All who were reborn on Calvary are the children of her love and she is the Mother of grace to all of them, but what mother is there that does not have her favorites? As Father LeJeune says: "Mary's love is boundless and her mercy extends to all. Nevertheless, she has her favorites. There is no one in the world for whom she prays more readily than for the religious of Mount Carmel and all who are affiliated to them, because she has a particular tenderness for them. The reason is that the religious of Carmel were the first to consecrate themselves to her. They are her eldest."

The special adoption by which, as the preface of the Scapular Mass says, we became "the sons of her choice" is the foundation of all the spiritual value the scapular possesses. And what a privilege this is! "And thou becamest mine." These words spring from the very depths of her tender Mother's heart. She brought us forth into the life of grace, wrapped us up in the garments of her special love and we became hers forever. We can easily understand the love that led Our Lady to wrap up her firstborn Son in the swaddling clothes, but that she should cover the ignominy of our spiritual nakedness is something that only her most merciful love can explain.

The thought that, from the moment she spreads her garment over us, her special love envelops our whole being should be the greatest force for good in our daily lives. It should inspire us with the profoundest sentiments of love and gratitude and bring us to dedicate ourselves to her in time and in eternity. Life itself is all too short to thank her. Her special love is like a ray of shining light which shows us her face in the midst of the heartless world of our banishment from God. Surely we can address her in the words of Eternal Wisdom: "Her ways are beautiful ways: and all her paths are peaceable" (Prov. 3:17).

A mother's love is the most practical thing in existence. It is never satisfied with words but is always pouring itself out on someone. Mother-love is also capable of the greatest sacrifices; it is born in suffering and time serves only to increase its generosity and service. If this is true of the mother-love we have all experienced, what must be said of the love of her who became the Mother of Sorrows and the Queen of Martyrs for love of us? When we see her with the sword of Simeon plunged deeply into her heart, how can we ever doubt that her love for mankind is as practical as that of her Divine Son?

Since she became the Mother of men, she has never ceased to show herself a mother to all who have gone to her for help. He who is mighty has done great things to her; and she in turn, who is mighty through the power of her divine motherhood, has done great things for those who have sought her intercession. She has been the cause of our joy and will continue to be to the end of time.

Our Lady is the Virgin Most Faithful; she will keep her promise and, since she is heard because of the great reverence due to her as Mother, her Son is bound to hear the prayers which she pours forth in our behalf. Her love for us is invincible for it was cradled in the Sacred Heart of her Son. It is stronger than death itself, and the waters of contradiction and ingratitude can never extinguish it. She knows us better than we know ourselves. She sees us tossed, without any comfort, on the billows of life, and, in her great and tender mercy, she has stooped down to bring us the peace, the eternal peace, of her scapular promise.

The spiritual alliance of the scapular puts our lives and our souls in the safe keeping of Our Lady. Her overshadowing love draws us into her bosom and we find protection from all our enemies in her invincible strength. When Abraham found himself in the strange and dangerous land of Egypt, he said to his wife: "Say that thou art my sister that I may be well used for thee and that my soul may live for thy sake" (Gen. 12:13). Abraham feared that since Sara was beautiful the Egyptians might kill him to take her, so he found safety in calling her his sister.

Through the alliance of the scapular Our Lady has called us the "sons of her choice," that our souls may live and we may be well used for her sake. The dazzling splendor of her holiness makes her the terror of demons. She is "terrible as an army in battle array" against all the forces of evil that would molest us or attempt to snatch us from under the mantle of her maternal protection. And as Queen of Angels she can summon legions of heavenly hosts to our defense. When the king of Syria sent his forces to capture Eliseus, the prophet told his servant to "fear not for there are more with us than with him. And Eliseus prayed, and said, Lord open his eyes, that he may see. And the Lord opened the eyes of the servant and he saw: and behold, the mountain was full of horses, and chariots of fire round about Eliseus" (IV Kings 6:16,17).

The Queen of the Angels repeats those words to those who are clothed in her habit: "Fear not, for there are more with us than with them." She can summon legions of angels to our side and surround us with the power of heaven. As Daughter of the Eternal Father, Mother of the Word, and Spouse of the Holy Spirit, her prayer is infinitely more powerful than that of any prophet. Even the mention of her name is enough to confound the powers of darkness. When the Lord opened the eyes of the servant he saw that his master was not alone. Neither are the "sons of her choice" alone in the battle of life. The alliance of the scapular brings us the strength of heaven; while we are clothed in the habit of Our Lady, we are surrounded by the forces at her command. "All who see them shall know that they are the seed the Lord hath blessed" (Is. 61:9).

As long as we live our lives and finish our course under the sweet protection of her mantle, we have nothing to fear. Our path to heaven is made easy by her who crushed the serpent's head and shared the glorious victory of her Risen Son. Our Lady is the Gate of Heaven particularly to those whom she has clothed in the garments of her love: "Whithersoever thou shalt go, I will go; and where thou shalt dwell I also will dwell" (Ruth 1:16).

Genesis tells us how Jacob loved Joseph above all his other sons and, as a sign of his special love, he made a coat of divers colors for him. This particular affection which the father had for his favorite son aroused the jealousy of his brethren. They determined to do away with him and when the opportunity presented itself, they stripped him of his coat, dipped it in blood and sent it back to his father who immediately recognized it as his son's. Could the eye of Jacob have followed his beloved son into the fields and had his arm been long enough to save him from his enemies, his love would have prevented Joseph from being sold into Egypt. The ever-vigilant eye of our Blessed

Mother is always upon those who wear her habit, and where her eye is there also is the love of her Heart to save and defend us. The might of her love follows us and wherever we go and wherever we dwell it is about us.

The place of our adoption is Carmel which is totally dedicated to her. It is a land of great spiritual riches, a home where the prayers and good works of each are the spiritual inheritance of all. It is the glorious privilege of lay people to become a part of this spiritual family, to enter the blessed land where one comes to know Mary as our life, our sweetness and our hope and to participate in its interior life of dedication to her.

*Chapter Three*

# A Pledge of Everlasting Salvation

"In her is the beauty of life and her bands are a salutary binding" (Ecclus. 6:31).

It is the teaching of our holy faith that no one can merit the gift of final perseverance. We have no lease upon the state of grace, no insurance against its loss. It does not follow that, because we are in the state of grace today, tomorrow will find us the friends of God and heirs to his Kingdom. We carry our treasure of divine grace in the earthen vessel of a fallen human nature which is easily broken. To continue the metaphor, one might say that it has been broken ever since the Fall and that our personal sins have weakened its powers of resistance.

Even though the Good Samaritan has left us his medicinal grace to heal the wounds left by sin, He has not restored to us the gift of immunity from concuspiscence which Adam had and which insured the divine treasure of grace against loss. In our redeemed human nature, there is an inherent weakness which places sanctifying grace in constant danger of being lost. This moral weakness has led to the formation of bad habits and inclinations to sin which have their roots deep in our nature. Bad habits are not easily rooted out and, while they remain, the state of grace is in peril.

Another factor that enters into final perseverance is that of the time of our death. We could never merit that death will come when we are in the state of grace. This depends upon divine providence and lies outside the order of merit. Strictly speaking, a person could live for years in the state of grace and have the misfortune to fall into grievous sin. If death overtook him before he had a chance to go confession or to make an act of perfect contrition, he would be lost.

This doctrine of the Church disturbs our complacency and brings us to throw ourselves more and more on the mercy of God. He who made us knows what is in man: He knows the clay of which we are formed and has promised that if we rely upon Him we shall not be tempted above our strength. Moreover, He has given his word that if we use the means of salvation which He has left, the crowning grace of final perseverance will be ours.

One of the greatest means of final perseverance we have is devotion to our Blessed Mother. It is the constant teaching of the Church that devotion to God's Mother is not only a means but a pledge of eternal salvation. Those who shelter their weakness in the motherly Heart of the Mother of our redemption "shall draw salvation from the Lord." That Heart, into which the tenderest mother-love drew all the agony of the Passion and Death of our Redeemer, is a tower of strength for the weak. She is our life, our sweetness and our hope; in her we may find the beauty of eternal life. To whom shall we go for an assurance of salvation if not to her who, in order to save us, offered both her Only-Begotten and herself to the cruel death of the Cross? "It is not near the Cross," says St. Bernard, "that Mary is found but on it, nailed to its beams as Jesus is." She loves us with the same love she has for her First-born, and the double-edged sword that pierced his Heart opened wide her Heart that it might be the refuge to sinners to the end of time and the gate to heaven for those who hope in her. Her love embraces every child of Adam and there is no power that will snatch a soul from her protecting love. She was made to be the Mother of mercy, and her mission on earth and in heaven is not to judge but to show mercy and to open her pierced Heart wider and wider to the poor banished children of Eve who fly to her for help. The Eternal Father made her "full of grace" that her love might bestow it where justice would deny it. As St. Bernard says: "She is impetuous in mercy, she is resistless in mercy. The duration of her mercy is unto the end of the sinner's life. The broadness of her mercy is unto the limits of the earth. The height of her mercy is unto heaven. The depth of her mercy is unto the lowest abyss of sin and sorrow. She is always merciful. She is only merciful. She is our Mother of mercy."

If it is the property of God to be merciful and to spare, surely it is also the very nature of the Mother of mercy to pour forth her mercy even where there are no merits. The quality of her mercy is never strained; and the devil, into whose heart a ray of hope can never shine, is the only one excluded from her love. She sees in every soul, even in that of the most wretched, the image of her Son, and, if necessary, she would become again the Queen of Martyrs to save the least of her children.

Our Blessed Mother holds such a place in the economy of our salvation that some do not hesitate to state that devotion to her is a necessary condition of salvation. "They who are not thy servants, O Mary," says St. Albert the Great, "shall perish." St. Bonaventure repeats the same thought when he says: "They who neglect the service of Mary shall die in their sins." And again: "For them from whom Mary turns away her face there is not even a hope of salvation." St. Ignatius of Antioch, a martyr of the second century, writes: "A sinner can be saved only through the holy Virgin who, by her merciful prayers, obtains salvation for so many who, according to strict justice, would be lost."

If a lack of devotion to her is a mark of eternal reprobation, a constant love for her must be a sign of eternal salvation. Many spiritual writers state that devotion to Mary is a sign of predestination. St. Alphonsus Liguori says: "It is impossible that a servant of Mary be damned, provided he serves her faithfully and commends himself to her maternal protection." St. Anselm writes: "He who turns himself to thee and is regarded by thee cannot be lost." St. Antonine is of the same opinion. He says: "As it is impossible for them from whom Mary turns away her eyes of mercy to be saved, so it is necessary that they to whom she turns her eyes of mercy and for whom she intercedes to be saved and glorified."

The scapular makes us not only the servants of Mary but also the "sons of her choice." From the moment we are enrolled in it, we are dedicated to her in a special way and have a special claim upon her protection and intercession. The scapular is her garment of salvation; wherever it is, there is the shadow of her maternal protection and her redeeming love which disposes all things wisely and makes them work sweetly for the eternal welfare of those whom she has adopted through her habit. Her pursuing love will follow us to the end of life enabling us to live and die in the state of grace. In virtue of the alliance she has entered into with those who wear the scapular, she will never cease to do them good until they need her help no longer.

Let us not conclude, however, that the scapular is endowed with some kind of supernatural power which will save us no matter what we do or how much we sin. We might apply here what St. Alphonsus says about devotion to Mary in general: "When we declare that it is impossible for a servant of Mary to be lost, we do not mean those who by their devotion to Mary think themselves warranted to sin freely. We state that these reckless people, because of their presumption, deserve to be treated with rigor and not with kindness. We speak here of the servants of Mary who, to the fidelity with which they honor and invoke her, join the desire to amend their lives. I hold it morally impossible that these be lost."

A perverse, sinful will can defeat the "suppliant omnipotence" of the Mother of mercy. Even Christ had to admit defeat, for He extended his crucified hands all day to an unbelieving and contradicting people that refused to return to the loving embrace of his Sacred Heart. How often would He have gathered his chosen children into his Sacred Heart and they would not! But if we turn to Our Lady, she will turn her eyes of mercy towards us and show us the fruit of her womb.

It is clear from the words of St. Alphonsus that a certain measure of fidelity is required on the part of those who wish to gain the special love and protection of Our Lady. The very wearing of the scapular is in itself an act of devotion, and when it is done faithfully, it renders habitual homage to its Queen. "Other pious practices," writes Father Chaignon, S.J., "are attached to certain times and to certain places but the devotion to the scapular belongs to all time and places. Thanks to my little habit, wherever I am, whatever I am doing, Mary never sees me without seeing on my body an evidence of my devotion to her. Always and everywhere my scapular pleads for me, recommends me to her tenderness, tells her that I love her and that I confide all my interests to her maternal care." The constant, daily practice of wearing the scapular is, therefore, an act of faithful homage to Our Lady but, as St. Alphonsus adds, the desire to amend one's life is also necessary before we can be morally certain that she will be the cause of our eternal salvation. We should be careful not to place limits upon the mercy of her who is the refuge of sinners and the Mother of mercy. How few there are to whom she could say at the end of life: Well done, thou good and faithful servant! There are countless souls in heaven today who owe their imperishable crowns to the special intercession of Our Lady. There is a wealth of theology in a little story Bishop Sheen loves to tell: "St. Peter approached Christ and complained that he found souls in heaven who had no right to be there. The Savior looked at him and said: 'Peter, I am not blaming you, for no matter how well you guard the gate to heaven they get in: when you close the gate, my Mother opens the window.'"

In this age of measurement, we should beware of attempting to reduce our Blessed Mother's love for sinners to fixed formulas. The burning love of her Heart cannot be caught within the narrow limits of any definition or rule or be expressed in the ordinary words of life. "One," says Cardinal Newman, "would not give much for that love which is never extravagant." Every mother's love is extravagant simply because it is what it is. How often does it happen that a mother has more love and affection in her heart for the afflicted child or the black sheep than she has for the children who need her less! If the father of the prodigal loved his wayward son so much that he aroused the jealousy of the faithful one, why cannot our Blessed Mother love and save where others would hate and condemn? If she is Mother for the sake of sinners, why can she not obtain from her Son that strong grace which compels even the rebellious will and bends it at the last towards God?

St. Alphonsus addresses her in the following words: "Thou canst relieve the most wretched and save the most abandoned." And St. Hilary says: "Even though one has been a sinner, if he has been devoted to Mary, he shall not perish forever." Spiritual writers tell us that it was the intercession of Mary that brought about the conversion of the good thief. Up to his last moments he lived in crime and sin, and even on the cross he filled up the measure of his iniquity by reproaching Jesus. What about about his conversion? The prayer of Our Lady standing at the foot of the Cross won for him not only forgiveness but a place in heaven that very day.

During the course of history the miracle of Calvary has been repeated over and over again. Sinners, in whom scarcely a glimmer of faith remained, have been saved through the "suppliant omnipotence" of that same Mother who lives to save even the most wretched.

We read in the life of the Curé of Ars that when he entered the church one day he found a woman dressed in black, praying for her husband who had committed suicide. She was in great sorrow because he had been most negligent about his religious duties. The Curé approaching, leaned over and told her: "He is saved; he is in purgatory and we must pray for him. Between the parapet of the bridge and the water he had time to make an act of contrition. The Blessed Virgin obtained this grace for your husband because, even though he was irreligious, he sometimes joined you in your prayers at the May altar in your room. This merited contrition and final pardon for him." Between the bridge and the water the grace to repent came to that poor sinner in return for that spark of devotion to Our Lady, which no one but the Mother of mercy could even consider.

The history of the scapular devotion is full of examples of

this kind. When Our Lady sees her habit there are her eyes of mercy, and the warmth of her love may melt the frozen heart and win for her Son one who would otherwise be lost.

Mary may obtain the grace of repentance even for the sinner who has had enough love for her in his heart to wear her habit, even though he has not had the courage to turn away from sin. This is why St. Claude adds: "It is not enough to say that the habit of the Blessed Virgin is a mark of predestination. Because of the alliance which Mary contracts with us and which we enter into with her, no other devotion renders our salvation so certain."

"God's love," says St. Augustine, "never deserts us." If this be true of the love of God for the sinner, it is, in a sense, even more true of the love of Mary, for her love is that of a Mother. Even though we may desert her, she will never desert us. The scapular will always catch her eye of mercy and bring to her lips from the depth of her tender heart a suppliant prayer for our return. Of one thing we may be certain: her eyes of mercy will be upon those who wear her scapular and she will admit defeat only at the gate of hell. Since the beauty of life is in her, she will do all in her power to put life where she finds death, strength where she finds weakness, and beauty of virtue where she finds the ugliness of sin. The one thing we should fear most is to forget to call upon her and to remind her of her promise to save us from hell.

Christ told St. Gemma Galgani that He was the rag-picker of souls. He is forever picking souls from the filth of sin. Mary goes with Him lest, in his justice, He turn away from anybody.

Can she not also stay the hand of death that would find us unprepared? She is the Mother of divine providence and consequently she can dispose all things wisely and sweetly for the eternal welfare of poor sinners. Was not the hand into which the Eternal Father put the power of his divine providence formed in her womb? Did she not cover it with her kisses? Did it not wax strong under her tender care? Did she not close its wounds and wash it in her tears when the lifeless Body of her Son returned to her lap on Calvary? Who can doubt that she can stay that hand when it is about to strike the unprepared sinner until the oil of charity lights the fire of love in his heart? Had the bridegroom delayed just a few minutes, the foolish virgins who had gone in search of oil for their lamps would have been on hand to enter with him. Our Lady's wisdom will hide our foolishness, and if we trust in her, the crowning grace of a happy death will come before it is too late. It will be recorded in the Book of Life that "the Mother of Jesus was there" at the end to save and lift up one who remembered the sweetness of her name, the power of her mercy and the tenderness of her promise to those whom she clothes with the garment of salvation.

Another point to remember is that enrollment in the scapular brings us into the Order of Carmel to share its good things and to participate in its spiritual treasure of Masses, prayers and good works. In one of her letters to a friend, Celina Maudelonde, who had asked her for prayers for the return of her husband to the practice of his religion, the Little Flower writes: "I am glad you have been enrolled in the holy scapular. It is a sure sign of predestination; and moreover will it not unite you more intimately still with your little sisters of Carmel?" When the story of our salvation is known, perhaps it will be found that we have been granted the grace of a happy death through the prayers of our brothers and sisters in Carmel. "There is a second reason," says Father Schultz, C.Ss.R., "why those who wear the scapular will save their souls: they will never be without the help of prayer." The Mother of God showed a vision of hell to the three little children of Fatima and said to them: "Pray for sinners: remember that many souls are lost because they have nobody to pray for them." The sinner who wears the scapular has a whole worldwide confraternity praying for him.

On the morning of September 30, 1897, the Little Flower of Jesus lay upon her deathbed in the convent of Carmel at Lisieux. Her eyes were fixed on the statue of Our Lady and this is how she described her last night on earth: "Oh, with what fervor I have prayed to her! And yet it has been sheer agony, without a ray of consolation. Earth's air is failing me; when shall I breathe the air of heaven! I could never have believed it possible to suffer so intensely. I can explain it only by my great longing to save souls."

That night she died and they took off her scapular. Today it is still there in a little reliquary on her bed. And when one sees it one cannot help exclaiming: Oh, Mother of God, she too wore the badge of our confraternity! This is what those who make light of the scapular cannot understand: the awful suffering of that little girl, her whole life of suffering, her agony on that bed, belong to us. Her brothers and sisters in the Scapular Confraternity will not know the flame of hell. Dear Mother, no wonder you could make such a promise!

I can picture, hidden away in some convent today, another Little Flower of Jesus, wearing the badge of Mary's confraternity, living out her years in silent suffering for the souls of sinners. She is praying for those to whom we will teach the wisest lesson I know—to wear the scapular always. How rich and beautiful in the sight of heaven is the land of Carmel upon which Our Lady has showered so many blessings! What a consolation it is for the sinner who ploughs his furrow alone through this world to know that the whole white army of Carmel's Queen and Mother never ceases to pray that he shall be worthy to exchange his scapular for the wedding garment of heaven! In the prayers of the Scapular Feast, we come upon a few lines that express the confidence and trust which should fill the souls of those who belong to Carmel: "In Carmel, where Mary is such a gracious Mother, why should one ever hesitate? Wheresoever the Virgin Mother turns her eyes, there is always an abundance of grace and blessing."

Even though we have the assurance of Mary's special help and the support of Carmel's unceasing prayer to plead our cause before the tribunal of divine justice, we should not tempt even the multitude of Our Lady's tenderest mercies. Those who wear her habit should be the first to give her the homage of their whole lives and to call her blessed at all times. The scapular is not simply the mark of a special devotion to her: it is the sign of a life lived in her. During the French Revolution, when the reign of terror was at its height, sixteen Carmelite nuns were dragged from their cloister on Montmartre to be martyred. As they stood waiting for the cruel knife to end their earthly pilgrimage, they filled the air with a hymn to Our Lady which expresses the true spirit of the scapular:

"In thee I place my trust, O Virgin, day by day.
Be my defense, my guard, help me in thine own way.
And when my last hour comes to draw my latest breath,
Obtain for me the grace of a most holy death."

*Chapter Four*

# The Sign of Our Perfect Consecration to Mary

"May it be to them (all Carmelites) a sign of their consecration to the Most Sacred Heart of the Immaculate Virgin" (*Letter of Pius XII for the Seventh Centenary of the Brown Scapular*).

Devotion to the Mother of God is as old as the Church. One might say that it began when Christ called her by the sweet name of Mother. Her own prophecy that all generations would call her blessed has been fulfilled to the letter for the long history of the Church is full of her praises.

Like everything that comes from the heart, devotion varies from age to age. Love is always restless, moving and forever seeking new ways of expression. This is, of course, as it should be for where there is life there is always newness.

The history of devotion to Mary reveals great variety. Every age has sought to honor her in its own way and what is true of ages is also true of peoples and countries. East and West are still one in love for her. Devotion to her reminds one of a great unfinished symphony directed by the Holy Spirit.

The modern form of devotion to Mary is consecration. Pius XII consecrated the entire world to her Immaculate Heart and, by word and example, he has encouraged this form of devotion to her. In his letter commemorating the Seventh Centenary of the Brown Scapular, he asked all the branches of the Carmelite Order to see in it a sign of their consecration to Mary.

Strictly speaking, it is not correct to say that this form of Marian devotion is new except in the sense that emphasis has been put on it in our day. As a matter of fact, devotion in the old and true sense of the term always meant consecration, that is, complete surrender of oneself. And when the Holy Father asked all who wear the scapular to see in it a sign of their consecration to Mary, he simply focused attention upon the old and historical significance of the Carmelite habit or scapular. From the early days of Carmel its habit has been a medium of consecration to the Mother of God. Its oldest formula of profession was to God and to the Blessed Virgin Mary of Mount Carmel. The hermits on the Mount engaged in contemplation to honor her and the avowed purpose of their life was to imitate her. She was their sister and model. And as she kept the word of God in her heart and pondered it, so did they pass their days and nights in meditation upon the law of the Lord. It was their special devotion to her that earned them the honored title of "Brothers of the Blessed Virgin Mary of Mount Carmel." An old belief was that the Carmelite Order was actually founded to honor her; if this be true, Carmel has never been unfaithful to its divine purpose for all generations of Carmelites have called her blessed.

One might ask: what does consecration mean? For our present purpose it simply means making a thing sacred by surrendering it to God. The man becomes a priest by being taken from among men and dedicated to the service of God; the cup becomes the chalice by being withdrawn from profane use and given over exclusively to the service of the altar; the place is made sacred by being reserved for divine worship. From the moment of consecration the person, thing or place belongs to God in a special way. And since God became man through Mary and deigned to make her his partner in the Redemption, we may offer all to God through her. As St. Louis de Montfort puts it: "The most perfect consecration to Jesus is nothing else but a perfect and entire consecration of ourselves to the Blessed Virgin."

Consecration, however, should mean more than a formula

that is soon forgotten. What we pledge to Mary is not just the moment or even the day of our consecration but our whole life. We give her all that we are and all that we have in time and in eternity to become her property, if one could use the word. Consecration is total surrender, a complete giving up of oneself to her.

The scapular should be a constant reminder that we belong to her at all times and in all places and that she has a right to all our service. It is so easy to forget that we need to be constantly reminded of what we are and of the change that has taken place in our lives as a result of our consecration. We are not different from the people of old to whom God commanded Moses to address the following words: "Tell them to make to themselves fringes in the corners of their garments, putting in them bands of blue that when they shall see them they shall remember all the commandments of the Lord and not follow their own thoughts and eyes, going astray after divers things" (Num. 15:38). We too could forget, and the fringes of the Brown Scapular are there round our necks to make us always mindful of the sweet yoke of Mary we have taken upon ourselves.

Consecration, therefore, is more than outward conformity to certain practices of devotion; it involves the whole of our life, more especially the mind and the heart. When one thinks of a consecrated life, the glorious example of Christ and of his Blessed Mother comes to mind. Christ's whole life was spent for the glory of his Father. He came not to do his own will but that of Him who sent Him. Even when his human nature recoiled in horror from the bitter chalice in the garden, his prayer was: "not my will but thine be done." When the evening of his life came, He turned to his Father in heaven and confessed that He had sought only his glory upon the earth. The life that began in the crib and ended on the cross was one totally consecrated to the Heavenly Father.

The life of the Blessed Mother was a perfect replica of that of her Son. Her words to the Archangel give us the key to her entire life. She was always and everywhere the handmaid of the Lord and she lived to do his will. She kept every word that was spoken to her in her heart and made her life the incarnation of the divine will as she knew it. When she told the waiters at the wedding feast to do what her Son would tell them, she revealed the secret of her own life and taught all of us the true meaning of the consecrated life.

Let us not think for one moment that a consecrated life after the example of Christ and his holy Mother is too much to ask of us. Each one of us may say with St. Paul: "He loved me and he gave himself up for me." As St. Bernard puts it: "He bought the whole of me with the whole of Himself." Since his Mother was a helper like Himself in the work of the redemption, can we not say of her also that she bought each and every one of us with the whole of herself? She was all things to all men for she lived only to magnify the Lord and to rejoice always in Him. When she asks us, therefore, to give all we are and all we have to God through her, she is just asking us to follow her example.

Consecration to Mary brings an added burden to our shoulders; but where there is true love, it is a glorious privilege to serve. The proud boast of St. Paul was that he was the servant of Jesus Christ; and he challenged any power to separate him from the love of God that is in Christ Jesus. Our proud boast should be that we belong in a special way to Mary and that the service of our entire life is all too small a return for what she has done for us.

What keeps us back sometimes from making a complete surrender of ourselves is our ignorance of the true purpose of life. We were not made for ourselves but for God and we can achieve true greatness and nobility only by living for God. Experience shows that human life must be given to someone or to something and that if we do not offer it to God, it becomes the slave of some low passion. "The men of the world," says St. Ambrose, "have as many masters as they have passions. Immodesty comes and says to them, you are mine, because you covet sensual pleasures. Covetousness says, you are mine; for the gold and silver you possess are the price of your liberty. All the vices come and say, you are mine." Every man born into this world serves some master and offers his life on some altar. And if our master is not God, it is bound to be some low passion that makes us its slave.

How uplifting it is for us to know that Mary, the Queen of Heaven, has said to each of us: thou art mine. The special adoption that is ours through the consecration of the scapular may be expressed in the words of Ezechiel: "I passed by thee and saw thee...and I spread my garment about thee, and I entered into a covenant with thee...and thou becamest mine" (16:18).

To become "hers" in deed as well as in name we must first of all strive to cultivate her spirit, for it is the spirit and not the letter that vivifies and gives meaning to our life. "If any man," says St. Paul, "have not the spirit of Christ, he is not his" (Rom. 8:9). The same applies to Mary: if we have not her spirit in us, we have no part with her and our consecration to her loses its meaning. We should all take to heart the counsel of the Venerable Michael of St. Augustine: "May Mary's spirit be in us all, that by that spirit we may live."

There is no need to say that the spirit is the deepest force in us; for not only is it rooted in the soul but it bends all the powers of the soul in a certain direction and makes them means to an end. It governs mind and heart, and through them becomes life and action. If, therefore, the spirit of Mary is in us, it gives a new meaning to life and converts all we do into the service of her and of her Divine Son. It lifts us above the passing things of time, lending vision, beauty and eternal value to even the smallest actions. It gives light to our minds and makes her beautiful ways ours. The spirit that rejoiced only in God is sure to transform our heart, bringing us to love what she loved and to hate what she hated. Consecration puts a seal upon the heart but if the spirit of Mary is not in it, it is not clean and the seal will soon be broken. The clean, unspotted heart is the only one that is worthy of the Immaculate: it is created in us by living in her spirit day by day.

If we are to cultivate the mind and heart of Mary, we must be faithful to the dying command of her Son to behold her. She is "the mirror of fashion and the mold of form" for every soul that is consecrated to her; and if we do not look into that mirror and mold our life accordingly, we are certain to lose sight of our ideal. Every wearer of the scapular should follow the counsel of the great Carmelite, Bostius: "May the loving memory of Mary accompany you day and night, wherever you are, wherever you go, in whatever you do. May it be part of your conversation, your recreation, your sorrow and your rest... You are indeed my heart and my soul, O Virgin Mother."

If consecration to Mary is to be a power for good in our daily lives, it must show itself in a sense of filial piety which will keep her in our minds and hearts. As her chosen sons, our attitude towards her should be that of her First-born who lived with her, obeyed her, leaned upon her and grew up in wisdom and grace under her motherly guidance and protection. It is an abiding sense of being "hers" that will enable us to live our consecration to her.

The scapular should be a constant reminder of the obligations we have taken upon ourselves. Its wearer is doubly clothed; for at Baptism he is clothed with the white robe of baptismal innocence which he is commanded to carry unspotted to the white Throne of God, and at the time of his investiture in the scapular he receives the brown robe of Mary which reminds him of his obligation to clothe himself with the virtues of the Blessed Mother. If Christ, says St. Bernard, is our garment, she too should be visible in our person and we should reveal her virtues in our conduct. No one should ever see the scapular without seeing something of Our Lady in its wearer. The consecrated life should always bear the good fruit of love, charity, kindness, meekness, gentleness and prayerfulness; it should be the bearer of Christ to others. "Mary gave us Christ," says Bossuet, "and we should see to it that in giving ourselves to her we give her back another Christ." When Christ lives again in us and is visible in our daily lives, our consecration to Mary, his Mother, is all it should be.

The saintly monk of our own time, Dom Marmion, was deeply devoted to Mary and after Holy Communion, while Christ was present in his soul, he would re-consecrate himself to her by simply saying: Mother, behold thy son. It is when Christ lives in us and abides with us that we are the sons of his Mother. It is the living image of Christ that makes the consecrated life. And there is no better place to find it than in the life of his Mother.

How beautifully all we have written about consecration to Mary may be expressed in the words of Ecclesiasticus: "Put thy feet into her fetters and thy neck into her chains. Bow down thy shoulder and be not grieved with her bands. Come to her with all thy mind, and keep her ways with all thy power. Search for her and she shall be made known to thee and when thou hast gotten her, let her not go: for in the latter end thou shalt find rest in her, and she shall be turned to thy joy. Then shall her fetters be a strong defense for thee, and a firm foundation, and her chain a robe of glory. For in her is the beauty of life and her bands are a healthful binding. Thou shalt put her on as a robe of glory and thou shalt set her upon thee as a crown of joy"(6:25-32).

Her fetters and chains are all bands of love that bind us to God in her.

*Chapter Five*

# Our Affiliation with the Order of Carmel

"I have brought you into the land of Carmel to eat the fruit thereof, and the best things thereof" (Jer. 2:7).

When we think of the many pitfalls along the way to heaven and remember our own blindness and weakness, it is consoling to know that we may travel the lonely path enveloped in the special love of God's Blessed Mother. Wherever her scapular is, there is her watchful eye to guide our faltering footsteps. It turns her eyes of mercy towards us and drives our hellish foes far from us, and in the strength of the grace her love obtains, we press forward to the gate of heaven.

Mary's special protection in life, in death and after death is not the only spiritual value the scapular possesses. Both the order and the Church have opened their spiritual treasures to endow it. From the time of our enrollment in the scapular we share in all the Masses, prayers and good works of the entire order; the Church has made it her great sacramental.

It is interesting to recall how the scapular, which is the habit of the religious of Mount Carmel, found its way outside the order to carry its spiritual benefits to those in the world. The century in which the Carmelite Order came to the West was the age of medieval splendor. It was an age in which the great religious orders rendered outstanding service to the Church by preaching their particular devotions. The Dominicans preached the Rosary; the Franciscans, penance; and the Carmelites, their devotion to Our Lady of the Scapular. These devotions soon became popular and in the course of time they formed a bond of unity with the orders, which was responsible for the rise of confraternities and third orders. Those who wished to be affiliated to the Dominican Order were devoted to the Rosary; those who wished to be identified with the Franciscan Order wore the cord of St. Francis and practiced penance; and those who preferred the Carmelite Order wore the habit in miniature form and were devoted to Our Lady of Mount Carmel.

The letters of affiliation which these men and women received from the order entitled them to a share in its Masses, prayers and good works and, in some cases, gave them the right to be buried in the habit. Soon they came to be known as brothers and sisters of the Brothers of Our Lady.

The third order came into existence later, although we do not know the exact date of its inception. The Bull of John XXII, dated July 8, 1318, proves that it was in existence before this date.

One might ask what the difference is between the confraternity and the third order. If members of both organizations share the same promise and are affiliated to the same order, what difference could there be? In his little work on the third order, Father O'Shea, O.Carm., explains the difference very clearly: "The purpose of the third order," he writes, "is something very definitely in advance of the aim of the confraternity. The confraternity admits to participation in the privileges of the order by what may be called affiliation. The person so admitted is not and cannot be called a member of the order. He shares in its spiritual life and privileges but he does not in any sense live the life of a Carmelite, neither is he bound to the observance of the counsels of perfection nor of those other means which we must make use of who are called by God to the interior life of the order.

"The Carmelite Order is for the members of the confraternity a great external aid to salvation by helping them with its prayers and good works and by affording participation in the indulgences and spiritual privileges granted to it by the successors of St. Peter. It regards them as its children who are especially beloved by our Blessed Lady. On the other hand, the third order, as the name indicates, gives an actual membership of the order and carries with it the obligation of living according to a rule which involves to a certain extent the practice of the evangelical counsels.

"What membership of the third order does therefore imply is that it places one in a better and more secure way of serving God and of attaining to eternal salvation. This is the great outstanding advantage of membership of the third order; it gives the whole reason for its existence, which is to enable people living in the world to follow to a degree suitable to their state in life the Carmelite rule of St. Albert."

By the fifteenth century the third orders had become so important in the life of the Church that she saw fit to grant them canonical approbation. In 1452 at the request of the General of the order, Blessed John Soreth, Pope Nicholas granted to the Carmelite third order the same privileges and faculties he had already granted to the Dominicans and Franciscans, and the Third Order of Mount Carmel began its full canonical life. The rule which was written by Blessed John Soreth himself follows very closely the old rule of St. Albert and preserves the ancient spirit of the order. It has been revised since and supplemented by means of constitutions for the government of the third order, but its latest revision (1948) makes no substantial change in it.

There are two forms of the confraternity: the organized confraternity, which is attached to a church and has officers and members just like any other parish organization; and the unorganized confraternity, to which all who are enrolled in the Brown Scapular belong.

Few wearers of the scapular realize what their association with the order through membership in the third order or the confraternity means in terms of spiritual benefits. The Carmelite Order is the spiritual family of our Blessed Mother. It is made up of the first, second and third orders. As an order that has given countless saints to heaven it has, to speak humanly, a certain standing in the sight of God, and the long centuries of existence have left it with a spiritual treasury of merits that must be pleasing in the sight of God. Membership in even the unorganized confraternity makes us a part of that great family of Mary and entitles us to share in all the Masses, prayers and good works of its members. This is something the world cannot understand; its policy is "an eye for an eye and a tooth for a tooth," and all that it has is too little for itself. But since love is the bond that binds all together in Carmel, charity is the guiding principle of its life. For hundreds of years the Brothers of Our Lady have persevered in prayer with her for all who wear her holy habit; love for her has led them to bear each other's burdens, to support each other on the way to heaven.

This thought, that we have a spiritual family behind us to sustain us by its never-ceasing prayer, is one of the great, strong props of our spiritual life.

What a mighty volume of prayer it is that goes up to the throne of God from Carmel! Long, indeed, is the litany of Carmel's saints; and those who have joined their Queen in heaven cannot forget those here on earth whom they see wearing the same habit and living in the same faith as they did. The Little Flower promised to spend her heaven doing good upon earth; the roses of her love are bound to fall in the greatest profusion upon those who belong to her beloved Carmel. She is just one among the many Carmelite saints who are spending their heaven praying for the wearers of the scapular. The united prayers and good works of the whole order here below must also speak most eloquently on our behalf. The prayers of St. Teresa and her nuns retarded the Protestant Reformation and saved the faith for millions of souls. This is just a single instance of how powerful the prayer of Carmel is to move heaven. Hands lifted up in prayer are the most powerful hands outside heaven; they succeed when all else fails.

When we feel the need of moral and spiritual support, we often ask our friends to say a prayer for our intention. When we belong to even the confraternity, we have thousands and thousands of brothers and sisters in Carmel praying for us always; and when we are dead and forgotten by our nearest and dearest, they will continue to intercede for us until we reach the gate of heaven and the arms of our Blessed Mother.

What profound charity there is in the prayer which the order offers for those who have put on the habit: "Look, O Lord, on this thy flock which, having cast aside the world and the desires of the flesh, finds refuge in its humility under the wing of thy protection. Shield these devout souls with the sign of thy invincible Cross and fill them with the interior virtue of our holy order that they may be adorned by faith, strengthened by hope, and inflamed by charity. Inasmuch as they have renounced Satan and sought Thee as their only Spouse and true Father, pour over them the dew of thy blessing. Pardon all their sins, strengthen their hearts in the hour of temptation and keep their minds free from sinful desires, so that, stripped of all unlawful longings, they may seek after the Cross alone. May they flee the world like Magdalen and live a heavenly life here below that, one day, with thy saints they may enter into the enjoyment of the things the eye has not seen, nor the ear heard, nor the heart longed for. Through the same Christ..." (Reception, Carmelite Ritual).

In order to promote the scapular devotion and bring as many as possible under the mantle of Mary's special protection, Popes Clement VII and Clement X decreed that all who wear the scapular participate in a special manner in the fruits, not only the spiritual works of the Carmelites to whom they are united as a confraternity, but also in all the good done throughout the whole Church. Sixtus IV opened to them the spiritual treasures of the Dominican and Franciscan orders by granting them all the privileges, indulgences and favors which are granted to the cord of St. Francis, to the Rosary of our Blessed Lady or to any confraternity whatsoever, so that "they enjoy them as much as if they were really members of these sodalities."

There are many "good things" which Carmel shares with those who wear its habit, and we can well understand why St. Claude states that the scapular devotion "is the most favored of all

Marian devotions." How badly we need the help of Carmel! No matter how poor we may be our spiritual wants far exceed our material ones, and we can all say with the Psalmist: "I am needy and poor" (Ps. 69:6). When we reflect upon our spiritual poverty and remember how unworthy we are to plead our cause before God, it helps to know that we have the support of so many Masses, prayers and good works. Many a poor sinner is saved through the prayers of a good mother or kind friend. St. Monica's persevering prayer converted her prodigal son, and the only return she asked for so many years of prayer was a remembrance at the altar. Carmel is a prayerful mother that never forgets her children, and eternity alone will tell how many have gained heaven through her never-failing intercession for those who wear the habit of her Queen.

The Church has also been most generous in granting indulgences and privileges to scapular wearers; and even today many plenary and partial indulgences may be gained from its devout use.

*Chapter Six*

# The Carmelite Way

"May they (Carmelites) all see in this keepsake of the Virgin herself (scapular) a mirror of humility and purity; may they read in the very simplicity of the garment a concise lesson in modesty and simplicity; above all may they behold in this same garment, which they wear day and night, the eloquently expressive symbol of their prayers for divine assistance... And certainly this most gentle Mother will not delay to open, as soon as possible, the gates of heaven for her children who are expiating their faults in purgatory" (Pius XII).

When God wanted Moses to build the Ark, He called him to the mountain, showed him a plan and commanded him to follow it accurately. Our vocation summons us to another mount—Carmel—where we are shown the pattern of life Our Lady of Mount Carmel wishes us to follow. She is the living pattern of all who live in Carmel with her. As Merton puts it; "if Elias stands as the model of all Carmelites, there is another and more ideal figure than that of the prophet, the figure of the Blessed Virgin Mary of Mount Carmel, who, even more than Elias, embodies in herself the perfection of the Carmelite ideal. Where in Elias we see at once the zeal and weakness of the prophet, his greatness and his imperfections, in Mary we see a sanctity that is beyond prophecy and beyond conflict, hidden in perfect humility and in ordinariness."

From the moment we are clothed in her habit, we should open our minds and hearts to her asking her, day by day, to show herself a Mother to us and to form the living image of her Son in us. As Blessed Edith Stein writes: "Just as grace cannot accomplish its work in souls unless they freely open themselves to its influence, so also Mary cannot fully realize her maternity unless one freely entrusts himself to her... She can form to her own image those who belong to her."

As we enter her blessed land of Carmel to eat the fruits and the good things thereof she addresses us in the words of Ecclesiasticus: "I am the mother of fair love, and of fear, and of knowledge, and of holy hope. In me is all grace of the way and of the truth: in me is all hope of life and of virtue. Come over to me all ye that desire me; and be filled with my fruits. For my spirit is sweet above honey: and my inheritance above honey and the honeycomb."

Addressing Christ, John of St. Samson said to Him: "Nothing brings before our eyes in a better way thy humanity and divinity than that which Mary has done outwardly and inwardly by deeds, words and the conduct of her whole life. She is a most lifelike representation of Thee, a copy of Thee to the extent that when we understand her perfections we understand Thee; we behold thy goodness in hers, thy love in hers just as we behold her goodness and love in thine. We must, therefore, contemplate her in her exterior and interior goodness as we do Thee and in a way that exceeds all natural speculation no matter how pure, simple, exalted and fruitful it may be. But if that which one sees in her transcends all understanding and comprehension, how much less can one understand what is hidden in her! Such things must be admired, revered and contemplated in the delightful quiet of an unspeakable, profound and secret silence. To gaze on them is to be ravished and spellbound because in her we behold the deepest revelation of Thyself."

Mary is all this and more. She is the living image of Christ, the deepest and most beautiful revelation of Him to the poor banished children of Eve. She is the first fruits of the Redemption, the first and greatest of the redeemed in whom one finds God's original design for human living in all the splendor of original justice. She is the prototype of the perfect Christian and of the Church. It was surely with her in mind that John compared the Church to a woman clothed with the sun, the moon under her feet and a crown of twelve stars about her head. In the words of Chesterton: "She sums up all the Church has to say to humanity." And as Boulgakoff (Russian) puts it: "It is in her that the secret of primitive Christianity as well as that of the Gospel of the Spirit (St. John's) lie hidden." Centuries ago Origen stated that no one can understand the Gospel of John who has not leaned on the breast of Christ and taken Mary for his Mother.

Carmel took her for its Mother and its first rule is to behold her in the radiance and splendor of her virtues. Since she is the Mother of all and the world's first love, all are devoted to her and call her by the sweet name of Mother. But in the mirror of Carmel's history certain features of her life are reflected which form what one might call "the Carmelite way."

Carmel began near the fountain of Elias and found its inspiration in the great prophet of Carmel. As Mary emerged from the shadows of history they found in her the perfect realization of their ideal of prayer and contemplation. It was not without reason that they were called the "Brothers of the Most Blessed Virgin Mary of Mount Carmel." In imitation of her they pondered the word of God in their hearts which they purified every day in the hope of eternal union in heaven. The *Institutes of the First Monks*, which is one of the oldest documents on Carmelite spirituality, defines its vocation in the following terms; it is "to offer God our hearts holy and free from every stain of actual sin and to taste in our hearts and to experience in our minds not only after death, but in some measure in this mortal life, the power of God's presence and the sweetness of supernal glory."

The spotless purity of Mary became the pearl of great price which she hid in the land of Carmel and which every generation of Carmelites had lived to find. Her immaculate purity led her to consecrate all her love to God and it gave her life a singleness of purpose that made her soul the living image of Christ. It became fruitful in every virtue and she has become the joyful Mother of many.

Mary has inspired all generations of Carmelites to offer God the sacrifce of the clean heart. Their holy ambition was not simply to avoid sin but to purify their hearts of every attachment to creatures. They knew that a divided love is unworthy of God and it was their desire to love Him with their whole hearts that urged them to cleanse themselves from every attachment. Since this purification of soul must be accomplished before one can enter heaven, one can see why the scapular devotion is intimately bound up with release from purgatory.

In this sex-ridden age when the virtues of purity, chastity and modesty are not only neglected but despised, one wonders what the future holds for society. It was devotion to Mary that refined the ways and manners of men, sanctified the home and exalted these virtues. The crude materialism of the present rejects them and pagan vice is finding its way back into the lives of men.

Mary's spotless purity made her soul the living image of the holiness of God and of the Church, the Spouse of Christ. Souls that follow her example reflect this heavenly splendor and prepare themselves for union with God. They see God even in this life and will see Him face to face in the next.

The scapular should be a constant reminder of the absolute purity of Mary and of our duty to imitate her. It should separate us from all that is not holy and inspire us to greater and greater purification of our lives. Blessed, indeed, are the clean of heart for they shall see God.

St. Luke records how Mary "kept all the things that were said to her pondering them in her heart." She made her heart the living library of every word that came to her from God; so much so that one may call her the Mother of the contemplative life. Carmel has always seen her in this light and the contemplative element in its long history is a reflection of her life.

St. Thomas calls Scripture "the heart of Christ": it reveals his Heart. Mary saw God in every sacred word that reached her. The same Holy Spirit that overshadowed her formed Christ in the body of Holy Writ. In the word she found life and unbroken union with God. Origen describes the Bible as "a cosmos of unlimited riches; a world of spiritual meanings, a new creation given to renew the first by renewing its significance. It is the Word re-creating the world in his own image."

The first glorious re-creation of the word was Mary who was more blessed in how she heard and kept it than in her conception of the Second Person of the Trinity. Like a seed planted in her soul it grew like the grain of mustard seed to be the greatest of all living things; and when the time came for her to say "be it done unto me according to thy word" she had already conceived the word in her heart. Her Immaculate Heart became the mirror of that of her Son: she was the one most like Him. "Behold," cried Dante, "the face most like Christ's; its brightness alone can prepare you to see Him."

The burning desire of her soul is to form her Son in us whom grace has made his brothers. How easy it should be to find Him in her. As the moon reflects the blazing light of the sun so does she his light which she mediates in the soft setting of a tender mother-love. As Pius X says, "this copy of Christ, the closest human nature can produce, is more suitable to our stature."

The way to become all God wants us to be is Mary's way. Virtue can grow from no seed that is not the word of God planted in our souls, covered with the warm love of our hearts and watered by the living water of divine grace. If we want to grow into Christ and live in Him we must read and meditate upon his word. It is in communion with it that we shall catch the glory of the Lord and be transfigured into new creatures.

Mary was so intent upon the word that it opened the depths of her soul to God and immolated her whole being to his will. Her words "behold the handmaid of the Lord; be it done unto me according to thy word" reveal how she lived in God's will. And because she kept nothing back, God gave her everything and the handmaid became the Queen of heaven. Sanctity invaded her whole being and He who is holy did great things for her.

Here again she is the model of total surrender to God. It is not enough to keep our hearts clean: they must be given to God that He may possess them. We die to self that we may live to Him and the life that is lived in his will is bound to become holy.

The consecration of the scapular has no other meaning than this. Carmel's habit is a symbol of surrender, of service and devotion. When it is receved we are reminded that it is a symbol of the yoke of Christ and of the burden that is light when carried with Mary's help. It makes us Mary's and the command she gives us is "whatsoever He shall say to you, do ye." We cast aside the world and the desires of the flesh and live to clothe ourselves with the new man who was created according to God in justice and holiness of life.

To live as Mary did seems to ask too much of weak, human nature and when we are tempted to think this way, we should recall the simplicity of her life. The Little Flower reminds us that Mary's life was "wholly commonplace" and she could not listen to the sermon that put Our Lady above the power of imitation of the ordinary person. Mary did the simple things of what we would call a primitive household in such an ordinary way that she attracted no attention.

The whole value of her work lay in the spirit of consecration to God's will that motivated it. As Merton writes: "In Mary we see a sanctity that is beyond prophecy and beyond conflict hidden in perfect humility and in ordinariness...The sanctity of Our Lady was great indeed, but so great that it cannot adequately be expressed in anything other than the ordinary ways of human existence. In this, as in so many other things, she resembles her Divine Son. Like Him, she was in all things human and ordinary, close to her fellow men, simple and unassuming in her way of life, without drama and without exaltation." And he adds "The true, sure instinct of the Carmelite saints has gone direct to the heart of this truth." The scapular is a symbol of this true instinct of the Carmelite saints, of simplicity and ordinariness. A holy man once said to me that the simplicity of the scapular would remind him of Our Lady even if he knew nothing else about it.

How valuable, then, is the counsel of Walter Hilton for all Carmelites when he says: "Give yourself as you are to God as He is." It is the life that we live day in and day out that glorifies Him and our love for Him should be so great that it cannot be expressed any other way. If we offer our life as it is to God, his holiness is sure to invade it.

Mary's life centered in the Eucharist and she was a very intimate part of it both as a sacrifice and a sacrament. It was due to her that Christ was able to give us his flesh to eat and his blood to drink. Knowing that He was both Priest and Victim, she prepared Him for Calvary and when the day of sacrifice arrived she offered herself in union with Him. Did she receive Him in Holy Communion? It could well be that she was in the Supper Room; for it was a custom that the mother should light the lamp that marked the beginning of the Passover. And since she lived in John's house and the Beloved Disciple surely did as Christ commanded when He said "Do this in commemoration of me," one may take it for granted that she received her God and her Son in the sacrament.

The Living Bread transformed her life and drew her to Himself. If Paul could say "I live, now not I, but Christ liveth in me," how Christ must have lived in the Mother He loved so much! The great Lover of the Eucharist, the Little Flower, cried out "O Host sacred and divine, O Bread of exiles, it is not I that lives; my life comes all from Thee." After the death of her Son, Mary was the great exile of heaven and it was the Host, sacred and divine, that transfigured her whole being and raised her up in a glorious Assumption to the sublime altar of heaven where she lives with Him to make intercession for us.

True devotion to Mary will also show itself in love for the Eucharist and the sure instinct of Carmel has always recognized this. The giving of the habit is always associated, as far as possible, with a liturgical function and the monthly procession is always of the Blessed Sacrament. The rule recommends daily Mass and Communion.

The Eucharist is the sacrament of our union with Christ. In the words of Elizabeth of the Trinity, He wants us to be another humanity in which He may renew the whole mystery of his life here below. He wishes us to abide in Him as Mary did that He may draw us to Himself forever.

In fine, the scapular which originated as an apron should remind us that we are here to serve. Christ said He came to serve not to be served and Mary declared herself the handmaid. We, her children should live to serve others. Mary was a woman of action as well as of prayer; she crushed the serpent's head and is like an army in battle array against all the enemies of her Son. We must join forces with her. Her arms were all spiritual. Hands lifted up in prayer are more powerful than the hands that strike in battle; lives patterned on hers are more eloquent than words and the deeds we do in union with her are full of redemptive power. As we rise morning after morning let us ask her to use us today.

"In her is the beauty of life and her bands are a salutary binding"(Ecclus. 6:31).